Erotic Antiques

The publishers wish to express their sincere thanks to the following for their involvement and assistance in the production of this volume:

Art Editor: Tony Curtis
Photographers: Phillip Springthorpe
                   Stuart Barton
                   Cressida Pemberton-Pigott
                   Gordon Robertson
Editorial: Harriet Bridgeman
                   Eelin McIvor
                   Nicky Fairburn
                   Catriona McKinven
                   Kate Smith
                   Donna Bonar
                   Jacqueline Leddy
                   Frank Burrell
                   James Brown
                   Eileen Burrell
                   Fiona Runciman
Foreword: Duncan Chilcott (Bonhams, Chelsea)

A CIP catalogue record for this book is available from the British Library.

ISBN 86248-130-9

Copyright © Lyle Publications MCMXC
Glenmayne, Galashiels, Scotland

Typeset by Word Power, Auchencrow, Berwickshire
Printed and bound in Great Britain by
Butler & Tanner Ltd, Frome and London

Erotic Antiques

Annette Curtis

'Attic Room' by *Louis Icart*, etching and drypoint, printed colours, signed lower right. *(Christie's)*

Introduction

While the term erotic art itself is hard to define, it is clear that art of an erotic nature still remains popular and continues to stimulate interest with collectors and connoisseurs alike. When the subject of erotic art is referred to, most people will express an interest, some will giggle and only a few show distaste or total disinterest. Following on from this observation, most of the parties that express a genuine interest will ask 'Who collects erotic art?' The answer to this is just about anybody! Men and women of all ages, religions and races have amassed collections of erotic art around the world, and throughout history.

Art of an erotic nature has always been of particular interest to artists and art collectors, from the Bronze Age to modern times it is a subject that has been a constant in the artistic tradition.

Cave painting, executed around 1000 BC, has been discovered depicting primitive men and women surrounded by symbols of their life and environment which includes references to farming, weapons, boats and sexuality.

The Ancient Greeks, usually considered as the originators of our whole western civilisation, had a very well developed sense of beauty that appreciated and valued the pure joy of sex. Wall paintings in Etruscan tombs, decorations on pottery vessels and explicit sculptures depict amorous encounters, orgy scenes and well-known rampant Greek figures of mythology such as the shameless Satyrs and the Siles.

The erotic art of the Roman Empire can easily be seen through the Pompeian wall paintings of the 1st century BC which have been preserved for all time when Pompeii was buried under a river of lava after Mount Vesuvius erupted in 79 AD. These paintings decorated the walls of the brothels, and compared with the erotic art of the Ancient Greeks, the Roman art appears more primitive, being harsh and brutal.

During the Renaissance, both Michelangelo and Leonardo da Vinci produced erotic studies, and later Rembrandt and Hogarth did the same. An etching exists that depicts Rembrandt having intercourse with his housekeeper with whom he lived in his later years.

Today, the tradition continues with erotic subjects produced to satisfy the creative needs of the artist and the appetite of the collector. Therefore it is not surprising that the interest in erotic art today continues to be as strong as ever, with the market place being as varied as ever. Antique and modern erotic pictures, books, ceramics, objects and jewellery are available to the collector, whatever the size of his or her budget, and if the original is beyond reach, there are plenty of good reproductions about.

Most the the erotic works of art available to the collector are paintings, drawings and prints. The painting and drawings are either so exclusive that they are beyond the budget of most collectors, or else they are poor, mass produced copies of standard works that are not really worth bothering with. The prints, on the other hand, are both plentiful and more affordable. Prints after the originals, were often produced as limited editions, are very popular and should represent good investments. The works of Thomas Rowlandson, Choisy Le Conin/Franz Von Bayross, and Marcel Vertes are good examples of the plethora of highly collectable erotic prints. Rowlandson offers a comic vision of sex with a witty recognition of his own sexual desires, while in sharp contrast Zichy's etchings from 'Love' illustrates the whole range of human eroticism. The series, which consists of thirty-six studies, takes the beholder from the beginnings of puberty through to adult sexuality. Aubrey Beardsley's graphic erotic art is amongst the most widely known and reproduced, as well as being amongst the finest. This almost exclusively eccentric English view of late Victorian sexuality is clearly seen in the ever popular and widely praised subjects of 'Lysistrata' and 'Salome' illustrating the absurdity of sexual fantasy. Franz Von Bayros was an illustrator of erotic books who also

The Monk and the Dairymaid by *Louis Icart.* *(Christie's)*

MESSALINE

worked under the pseudonym of Choisy Le Conin, producing very imaginative and beautiful subjects in an elegant mannerist style. His women are tall and smooth, while the erotic scenes are always dignified, as seen in his illustrations to 'Fanny Hill' and 'The Arabian Nights'. Marcel Vertes was also a book illustrator, and is one of the more renowned recent erotic artists. His erotic illustrations depict sexual situations that express as much about the partaking characters as the situation itself. His view of eroticism has been called 'poetic pornography' by some, and can best be seen in its best-known expression 'Les Pays a Mount Gout' (Countries that I like). More topically, the work of an East European artist called Dimanov had his erotic works published in 1986 in 'When the flame and the rose are one'. This limited edition publication is an erotically thought-provoking piece containing signed etchings which are set to become collectable in the future.

Similarly, another modern illustrator's work has recently come on to the erotic art

'Messaline' a pen and ink drawing of a nude woman reclining on a day bed beside an erotic statue, signed and dated Demetrios, anno 1909, 11¼" x 8½".
(Bonhams)

market. David Wilde, who died in 1974, produced many highly finished illustrations for German publications. Most of these are sensitive, humorous studies of lovers in various sexual attitudes, while others are violently explicit scenes that portray a disturbed eroticism. Wilde's illustrations are worth pursuing in the future, especially the humorous subjects, such as the 'Private Diary', featuring naked judges in compromising bed scenes, or the limited edition of 'Nymphomania' portraying the faces of women with noses shaped as phalluses!

Amongst the most prodigious producers of erotic art were the Japanese during the nineteenth century. In sharp contrast to the Europeans, the Japanese had a free and open sexual morality, there was no discrimination against pornography and sexuality was regarded as a virtue. While erotic art in Europe had to be executed in secrecy and then supplied to a clandestine market, the Japanese artists worked openly, using their talents towards sexual education. This sexual openness, together with the traditional roles of Japanese women, resulted in very erotic art.

In Japanese culture it was essential to the happiness and harmony of her life that Japanese women knew how to refresh her companion. It has even been maintained that her only source of satisfaction was in satisfying the sexual needs of her male partner. Therefore, Japanese women were educated to fulfil that role from earliest times, and consequently young brides were presented with 'bridal books' from which they could learn what was expected of them. 'Pillow books' are also a part of this culture and were kept at hand in the bedroom to help stimulate the partners before sexual contact took place. Both these types of book were illustrated with colourful woodcut subjects depicting explicit erotic stories concerned with foreplay, oral stimulation and artificial penis use, and are very collectable today.

The Japanese ivory carvers also contributed to the art scene with erotic pornographic Netsuke. These small purse decorations are much sought after, and like the prints can be both erotic and humorous. Certain subjects are very popular such as sea shell carvings, that when turned up-side-down, reveal female genitalia, or dogs that are looking up in surprise and puzzlement as amorous tortoises mount them from behind!

Providing a contrast to the graphic erotic art of the Japanese is that of the Chinese. Their silk paintings are very pleasing and soft, without the frankness and large 'membrum virile' favoured by the Japanese. The Chinese approach is that of the voyeur giving the subject a titillating quality, and for this they are often prized more highly by collectors.

Similar in approach, but differing in technique, is the erotica of India. Most commonly encountered as miniature paintings on ivory, they are regarded amongst the most decorative of all erotic art types. It portrays a gentleness not often encountered in European or Oriental works, while avoiding the cold educational style of the Japanese. Hareem scenes or loving couples are accompanied by sitars, scented teas, love potions, and set with interiors decorated with carpets, ground beds or flora. The artists pay equal attention to the sundries in the scenes and the sexual encounter, thus softening the overall eroticism suggested in these small works of erotic art.

Objects are amongst the other most popular areas of erotic art collecting. These can be small secretive objects such as snuff boxes, card cases or tobacco pouches with false lids or secret compartments concealing erotic scenes designed to titillate the owner. They are very popular among collectors and so usually realise larger prices in the marketplace. Likewise, the carved bone or ivory phallus has also always been popular with collectors of erotic art, being either highly decorative dildos or amusing snuff mulls usually engraved with intimate love scenes. Many of the erotic objects are gentlemen's accessories which were very fashionable in the late eighteenth century, and remain equally amusing and risque today. A collector once showed me a hugely enjoyable and quite rare continental carved bone pipe tamper modelled as an upright and sober judge in full procedural robes. The robes had a door set in them which, when allowed to fall open, revealed a large articulated phallus. Erotic objects similar to this are great fun and are highly prized by collectors fortunate enough to obtain an example. Equally highly prized are the gold or silver half-hunter and full-hunter type pocket watches, favoured by gentlemen of the nineteenth century, which can either have an erotic movement or a case that hides a picture of an erotic encounter.

More recently, the acclaimed art form of photography was not long in discovering the erotic subject. Any visit to a photographic exhibition will reveal the large number of images entitled 'Nude Study' or similar.

However, at the turn of the century the stereo-photograph image was very popular, and lent itself to erotic subjects very well. These stereo-photograph images, which were produced in Italy and France, when viewed through a binocula style stereoscopic viewer, appear as very realistic three dimensional erotic scenes.

Erotic art, by its very nature and perhaps deliberately has to ignore conservative values. It must not offend or disgust, nor can it gloss over or hide. A good work of erotic art should demonstrate the beautiful, joyful elements of human sexuality and pure sexual enjoyment, while a poor work is simply not worth possessing.

Duncan Chilcott
Head of Collectors Department, Bonhams.

'The Jugglers' by *Thomas Rowlandson*, a fantasy based on *Callot's* phallic etchings of the Commedia dell' Arte.

Above

Curiosity: a Georgian lady looking through a keyhole, stippled hand-coloured engraving, published 1817 by *S.W. Fores*, 13½" x 10". *(Bonhams)*

Right

'La Source', a green-patinated and gilt bronze Art Nouveau clock, cast from a model by *Charles Korschann*, the rectangular pilastered niche on stepped base, with a gilt bronze maiden standing contraposto, 31cm. high *(Christie's)*

Right

A Charles Sykes bronze group, modelled as a satyr and bacchante sitting astride a mule reminiscent of a motorcycle, speeding across a wave-like base, mounted on green marble, 17cm. high, signed *Charles Sykes* and dated *1923. (Phillips)*

A good erotic miniature painting, of partly-dressed lovers on a park bench, watercolours on celluloid, signed *Johns*. 2¼" diameter. *(Bonhams)*

Right
A 19th century French bronze group, in the style of Carrier-Belleuse, with a revelling bacchante offering libations to a caryatid statue of Bacchus on naturalistic base, bearing the signature *Clodion*, 16¼" high. *(Christie's)*

Overpage
'A music master flying his instrument', after Thomas Rowlandson, watercolour and ink, 6" x 8". *(Bonhams)*

Right
19th century French silver patch-box
with carved ivory top, depicting an
amorous couple.

Below
French gilt-bronze lesbian figures,
circa 1900.

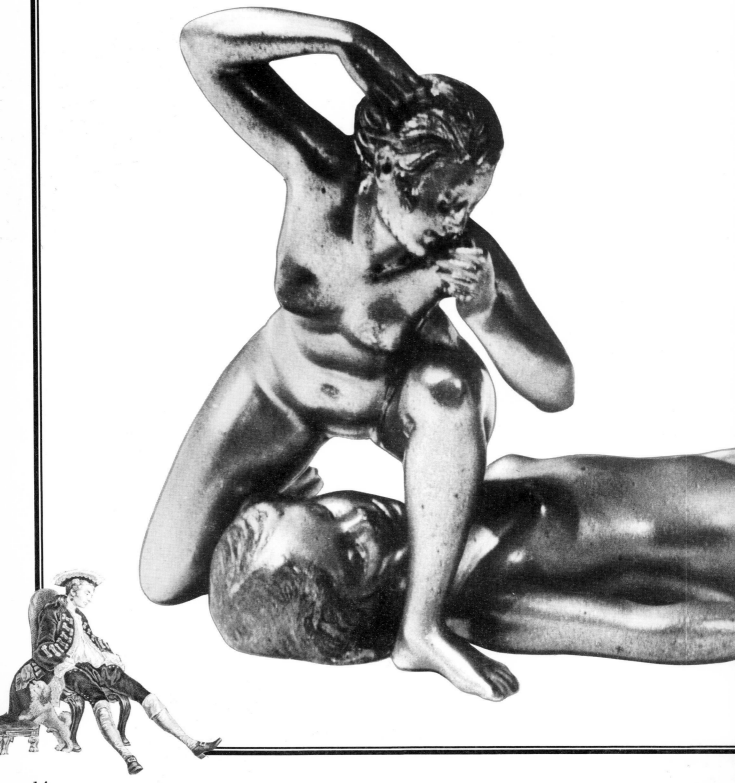

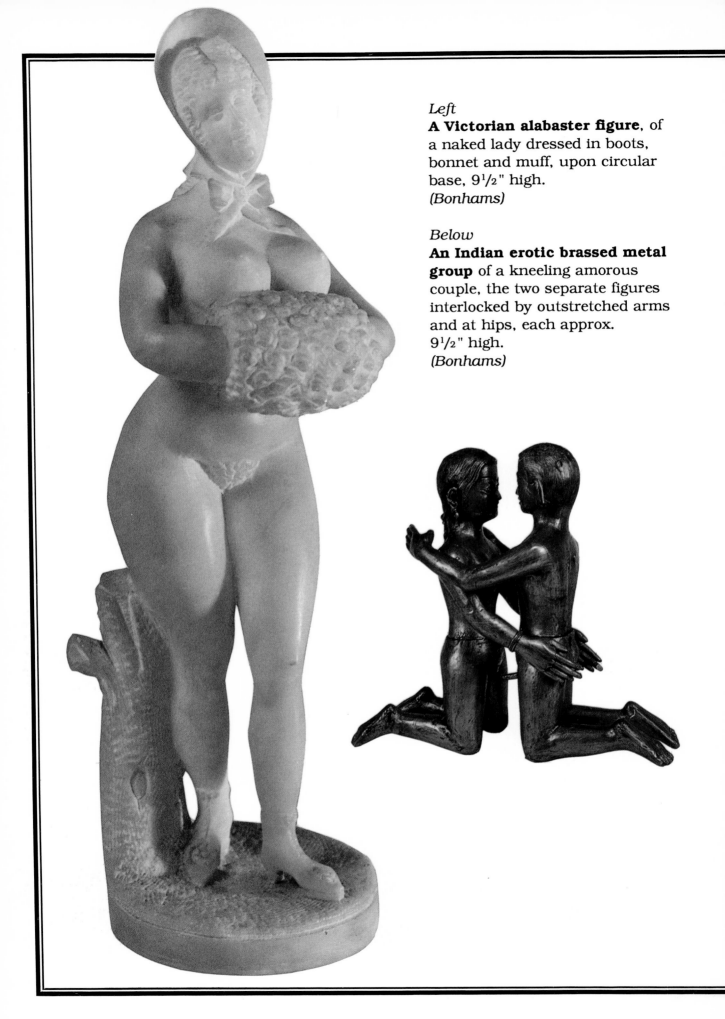

Left
A Victorian alabaster figure, of a naked lady dressed in boots, bonnet and muff, upon circular base, 9½" high.
(Bonhams)

Below
An Indian erotic brassed metal group of a kneeling amorous couple, the two separate figures interlocked by outstretched arms and at hips, each approx. 9½" high.
(Bonhams)

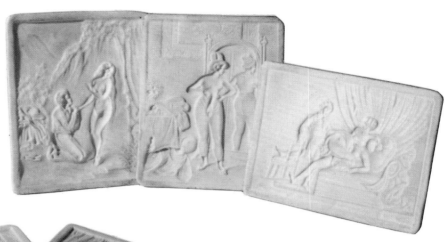

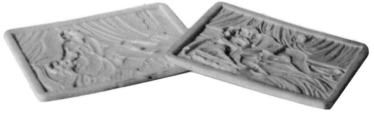

Above
19th century lithophane miniature panels depicting amorous couples and groups in interiors and lovers beneath a waterfall, various sizes, the largest 2¹/₂" x 2". *(Bonhams)*

Left
19th century continental porcelain plaque finely painted with an erotic scene depicting lovers al fresco, 5¹/₄" high. *(Christie's)*

Above
19th century gold cigarette-case with an engraved lid which can be lifted to reveal a curious seduction scene.

Right
Early 19th century patch box with painted decoration on both sides of the lid, the interior having a scene of love-making.

Far right
An Art Nouveau bronze vase cast from a model by *Louis Chalon* depicting a naked gilt bronze ice maiden projecting from one side, 45.5cm. high. *(Phillips)*

Left
Twenties figure of a young girl in décolletage by *Bruno Zach,* in bronze and carved ivory on an onyx base.

**Three lithophane minia-
ture panels** depicting
acrobatic lovers, a portly
gentleman with his
mistress and an amorous
couple surprised by a
frog, each approx.
3 x 2¹/₄".
(Bonhams)

An engraved topaz depicting an
erotic scene involving three
satyrs and a woman, the topaz
supported by two silvered metal
young satyrs upon oval base, 2³/₄" high.*(Bonhams)*

Rural Felicity or Love in a Chaise

Above
'Rural Felicity' or 'Love in a Chaise' by *Thomas Rowlandson (1757-1827).*
Left
Art Nouveau style gilt bronze reclining female figurine, 4¹/₂" long. *(Bonhams)*

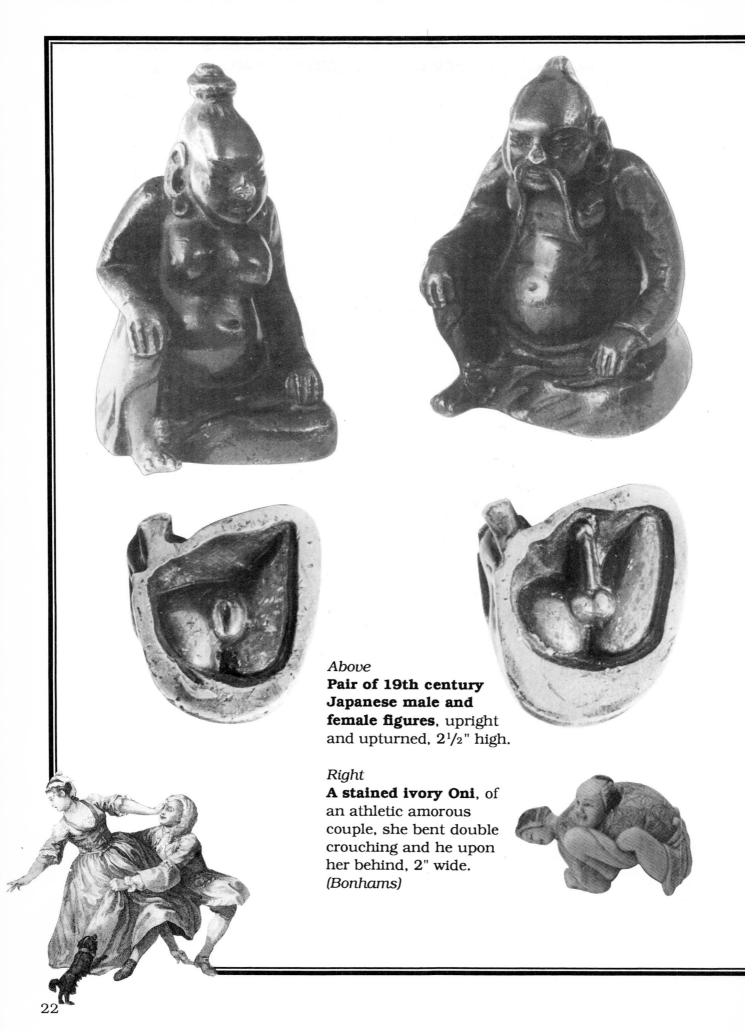

Above
Pair of 19th century Japanese male and female figures, upright and upturned, 2½" high.

Right
A stained ivory Oni, of an athletic amorous couple, she bent double crouching and he upon her behind, 2" wide. (Bonhams)

22

Above
Late 18th century Chinese carved ivory erotic scene, set in a 19th century frame.

Left
Chinese porcelain snuff-bottle decorated with a couple making love.

23

Left

'Spring Awakening', a bronze and ivory figure cast from a model by *Ferdinand Preiss*, of a maiden standing with her arms outstretched, wearing a short gilt skirt tied around her waist and with a silver-patinated cloak draped across her arms, 14½" high. *(Christie's)*

Below

A European bronze figure of a young woman in pantalettes and stockings embracing an outsized phallus, 9" high, signed on base *Zach 1914*, upon beige marble base. *(Bonhams)*

An Art Nouveau style bronze female figure of an exotic dancer, her swirling skirts opening to reveal the nude, upon hexagonal plinth stamped on base *Austria*, 9¼" high. *(Bonhams)*

AUBREY
BEARDSLEY.

26

Left
Print by *Aubrey Vincent Beardsley* (1872-1898)

Right
'Sacrifice', an ivory figure of a naked maiden, holding a shallow green onyx bowl above her head, kneeling on an oval ivory base, 15.5cm. high *(Christie's)*

Far right
A German enamelled cigarette case depicting a young woman wearing an off the shoulder dress and enjoying the amorous advances of her suitor in a boudoir setting, 8.7cm. high. *(Phillips)*

Far right
An enamelled cigarette case decorated with a naked girl sitting on a wall catching water from a spring, 9cm. high, stamped *935* *(Phillips)*

Above and right
A pair of famille rose plates, painted with lovers, the figures in unusual physical positions, the reverse with butterflies, 19th century, 8¼" diameter. *(Bonhams)*

Right
An ivory vesta case with engraved roundel to the front panel depicting an amorous couple, she lying on top, the man only partly visible, 1⅝" x 1". *(Bonhams)*

An Indian erotic wood panel, carved in high relief with an amorous couple upon an ornate canopied bed, 4¹/₄" x 3¹/₄". *(Bonhams)*

Left
Ivory pipe in the form of a black slave pleasuring his mistress. A satire of American Colonial life, German, mid 19th century.

Right
German commemorative medal with a nude woman harnessed to an erect penis representing an attack on the French occupation of the Rhine.

Below
A Lalique coupe calypso semi-opaque glass bowl, of shallow flared circular form, moulded with continuous bands of mermaids amidst waves, 30cm. diameter. *(Spencers)*

Right
Meerschaum pipe made by *Franz Hiess* of Vienna 19th century, with a carving of a nude woman.

Overpage
French erotic print of amorous young ladies and gentlemen in the 'roaring twenties', 9" x 7".
(Bonhams)

31

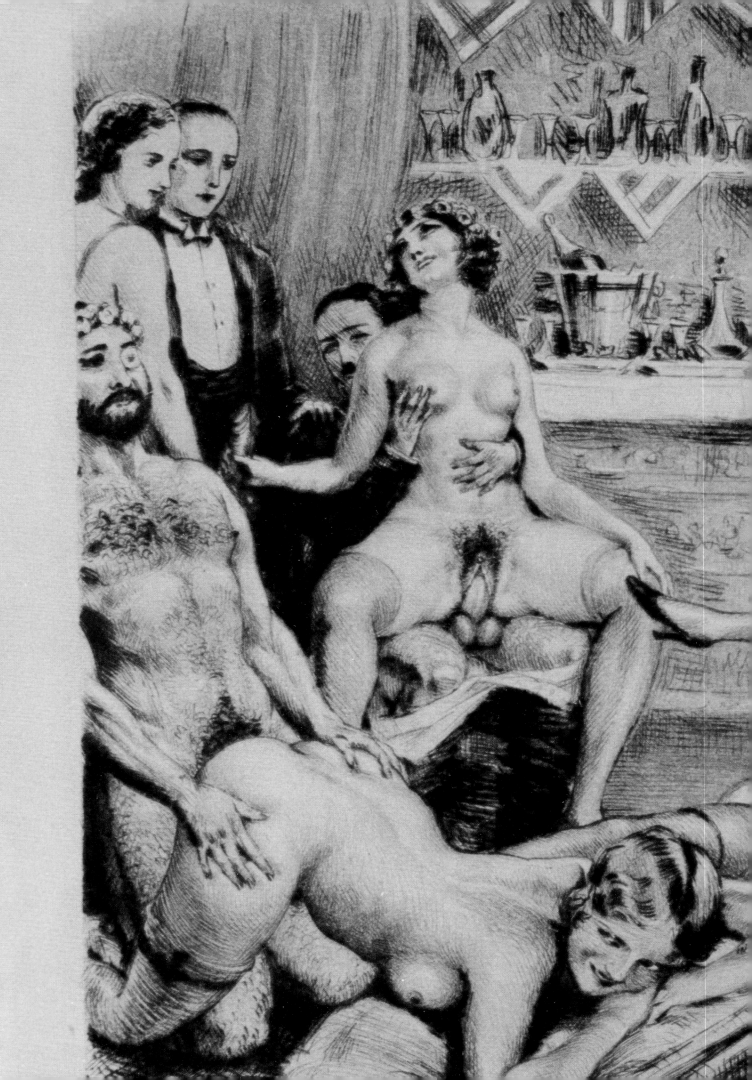

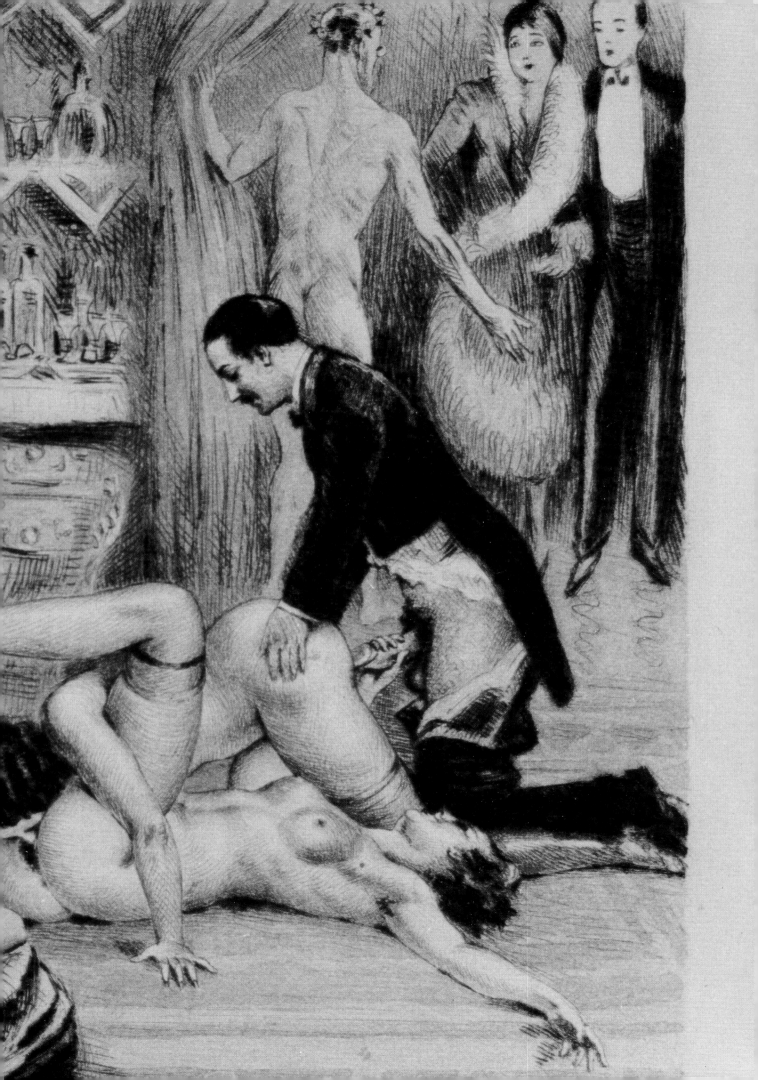

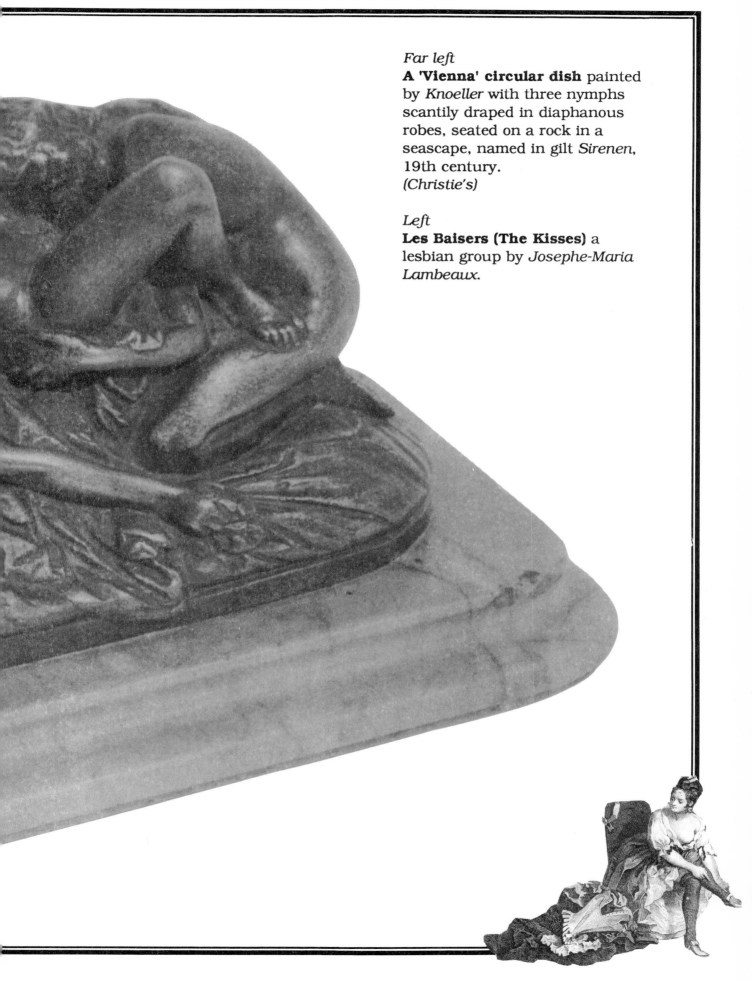

Far left
A 'Vienna' circular dish painted by *Knoeller* with three nymphs scantily draped in diaphanous robes, seated on a rock in a seascape, named in gilt *Sirenen*, 19th century.
(Christie's)

Left
Les Baisers (The Kisses) a lesbian group by *Josephe-Maria Lambeaux.*

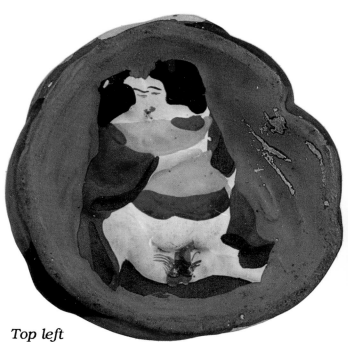

Top left

**A pair of rare 'Hatcher' blue
and white wine cups**, the thinly
potted bodies painted to the
exterior with a couple involved in
erotic activities upon a carpet,
2⅝" high, *Chenghua mark 1645*,
transitional period.
(Bonhams)

Top right

**Two Chinese painted plaster
seated figures** of a man and a
woman in brown and blue floral
kimonos respectively, each with
a moulded amorous couple upon
the base, each 2" high.
(Bonhams)

Bottom left

A Japanese erotic watercolour
depicting an amorous couple,
she below in a purple kimono,
he above in a brown kimono,
with ink on silk, 9 x 5½"
(Bonhams)

Bottom right

**A Chinese porcelain painted
and glazed tomato** opening to
reveal a cast, painted and glazed
amorous couple, she reclining,
he seated, 3" long.
(Bonhams)

A 19th century carved alabaster group of Cupid and Psyche, *after Canova*, the naked lovers embracing on a rock, 47cm. high.
(Phillips)

Right
An erotic Austrian bronze figure of a dancer, playing the castanets, wearing a detachable hinged cold painted dress, standing on a circular marble base, circa 1900.
(Sothebys)

Swiss watch decorated in neo classical manner with enamelled decoration and pearls inset in gold. The back opens to reveal a scene of love-making, circa 1800.

Above
A gilt verge watch
with concealed
erotic scene of a
monk and
courtesan by
Mauris à Geneve,
circa 1790, 53mm.
diameter.
(Christie's)

Left

An Art Nouveau gilt-bronze mounted ceramic vase by *Charles Korschann*, the greenish-blue glazed ground with a central gilded panel moulded with an Art Nouveau maiden holding a drape, 65.3cm. high. (Christie's)

Below

'Illusion' by *Louis Icart*, etching and drypoint, printed in colours, signed lower right with artist's blindstamp, © *Copyright 1940 by L. Icart N.Y.*, 50cm. x 23cm. (Christie's)

Above
An erotic scene of lesbian lovers, one wearing a large black hat, the other in leopard print stockings, black ink on paper, after *Erté*, 13$^{1}/_{2}$" x 9$^{3}/_{4}$". (Bonhams)

Left
'Nuit et Jour', a rare Lalique topaz glass clock, of disc shape, modelled in relief and intaglio with nude male and female figures, 14$^{3}/_{4}$" high. (*Christie's*)

41

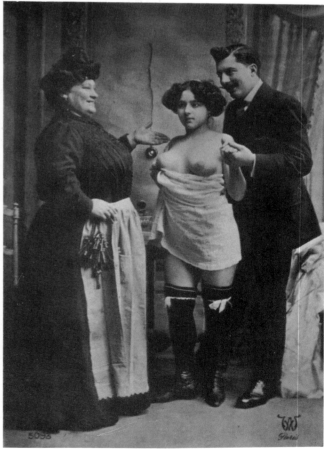

**Early 20th
century French,
'real photograph'
risqué postcards,**
circa 1905

43

A French pewter figure, of a young woman lounging in an armchair, with detachable dress, 3¼" high.
(Bonhams)

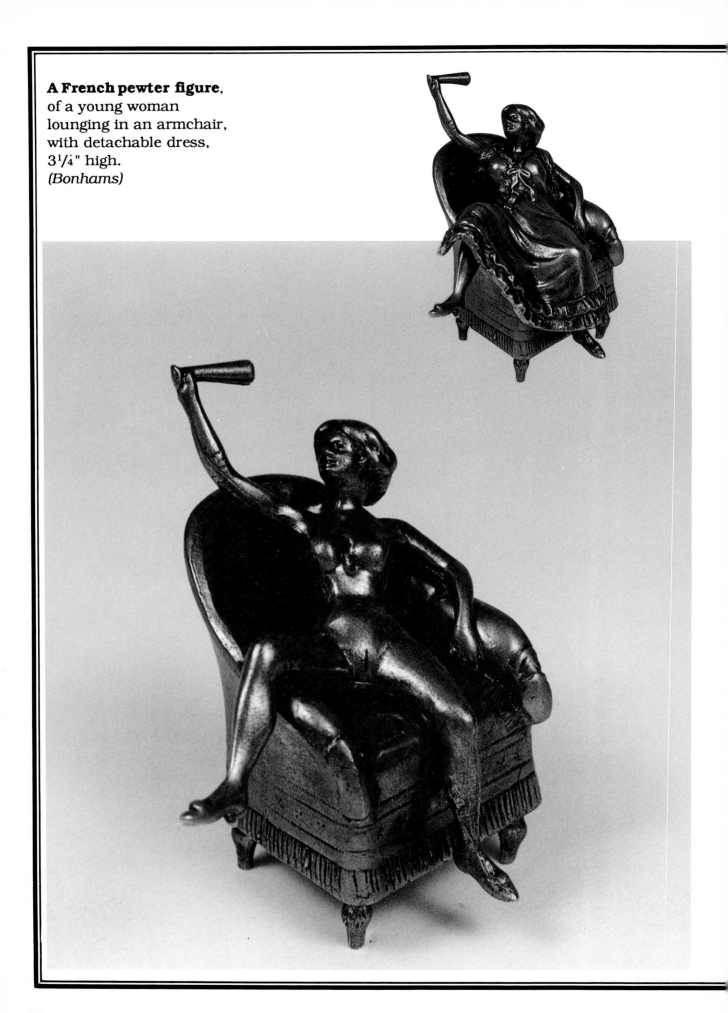

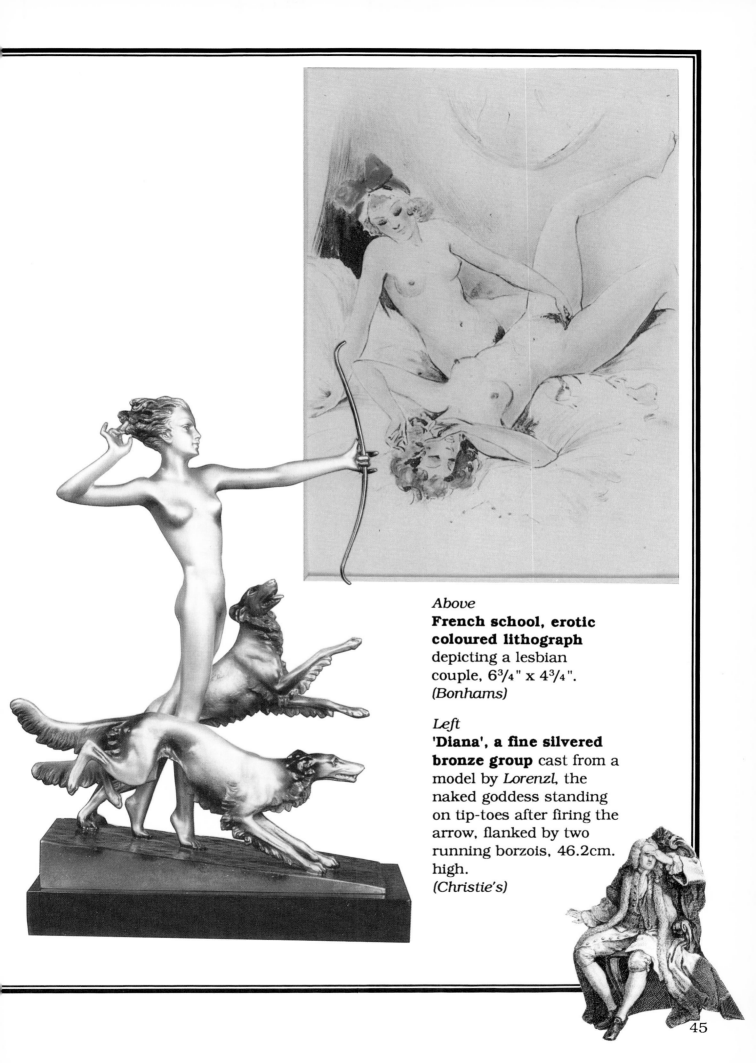

Above
French school, erotic coloured lithograph depicting a lesbian couple, 6³/₄" x 4³/₄".
(Bonhams)

Left
'Diana', a fine silvered bronze group cast from a model by *Lorenzl*, the naked goddess standing on tip-toes after firing the arrow, flanked by two running borzois, 46.2cm. high.
(Christie's)

Japanese medical figure, late 19th century, ivory. Used by the medical profession for coy ladies to identify their ailments.

Left
19th century Indian miniature depicting two lovers.
(Bonhams)

Below
A well-patinated ivory netsuke of an amah sitting beside a large octopus whose amorous approaches she tries to resist, signed in an oval reserve *Shuraku*, late 19th century, 4.3cm. high.
(Christie's)

Carved ivory netsuke depicting amorous couples
(Bonhams)

Above
Japanese erotic coloured woodblock print, 9³/₄" x 14¹/₄".
(Geering & Colyer)

Left
19th century carved ivory netsuke of an amorous couple.
(Bonhams)

Left

A French bronzed metal figure of a dancer performing the splits, her under skirts parting on base to reveal genitalia, 4½" long.
(Bonhams)

Below left

A German mid 19th century round papier-mâché box, the lid painted with a lady and three gentlemen in period dress standing beneath a tree, a false panel to the interior removing to reveal an erotic version of the same scene, 3¾" diameter.
(Bonhams)

A European erotic bronzed metal plaque, cast in high relief with two entwined young women with long flowing hair, 4¾" diameter.
(Bonhams)

A European cold cast bronzed metal group depicting an amorous satyr with a woman lying on her side, upon green and brown soapstone base, 5 x 2¾", signed *SM*.
(Bonhams)

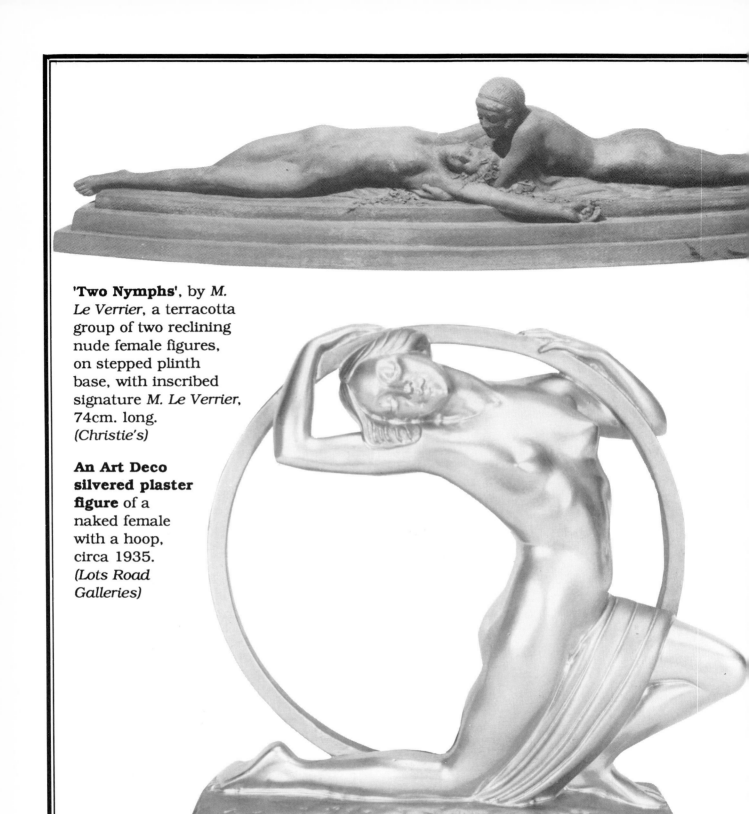

'Two Nymphs', by *M. Le Verrier*, a terracotta group of two reclining nude female figures, on stepped plinth base, with inscribed signature *M. Le Verrier*, 74cm. long. *(Christie's)*

An Art Deco silvered plaster figure of a naked female with a hoop, circa 1935. *(Lots Road Galleries)*

Right
A Royal Copenhagen erotic group 'The Wave and The Rock', of a man tethered to a rock, embraced by a woman rising from the waves, Copenhagen mark, 47" high. *(Osmond Tricks)*

Far right
Austrian carved ivory dildo, 1905-10, made by the *Wiener Werkstätte*, on a marble base.

Below
A large Art Nouveau gilt bronze jardiniere, cast from a model by *Ferdinand Faivre*, in the form of a large layered shell borne on waves and guided by a naked female amid aquatic foliage, 52cm. wide.
(Phillips)

Overpage
'The Intimate Bath', a Chinese erotic watercolour painting of a voyeuristic interior scene, 17" x 18".
(Bonhams)

Top left
Silver ring, probably by the French jeweller *René Lalique*, circa 1900, decorated with a continuous orgy scene.

Above
German Art Nouveau inkwell in the shape of an octopus and a mermaid, of gilt bronze and glass. Exhibited and listed by *André Breton* as one of the hundred precursors of Surrealism.

A Hindu wood panel
carved in relief with
the standing figure of
Parvati, with two
supporters standing to
attention behind an
amorous couple,
14½" high. *(Bonhams)*

Top right
**An erotic Indian bone
relief carving** of an
amorous couple, she
with her foot upon his
shoulder, 2¼" wide.
(Bonhams)

Right
**A bronzed metal oval
tea caddy**, the side
panels decorated with
an erotic scenario in
two parts, 6½" high.
(Bonhams)

Right
A Persian erotic oil painting on paper depicting two amorous couples upon floral rugs, inscriptions in ink, the illustration 8" x 4¼".
(Bonhams)

Below
An erotic Indian bone relief carving depicting an embracing amorous couple wearing elaborate headdresses, the reverse carved with scrolling leaves, 2½" long.
(Bonhams)

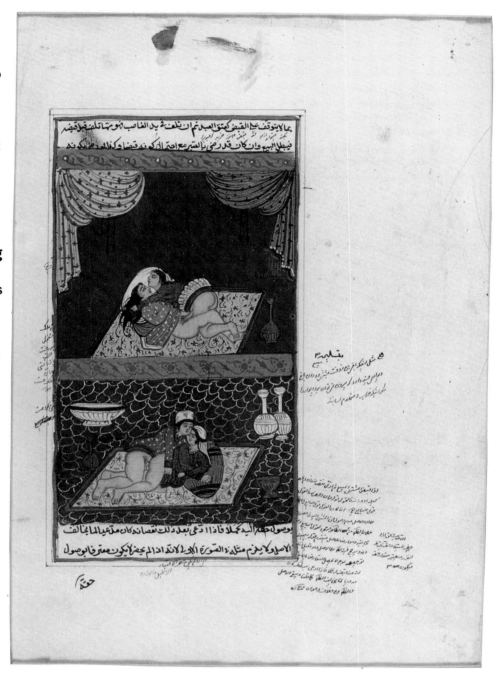

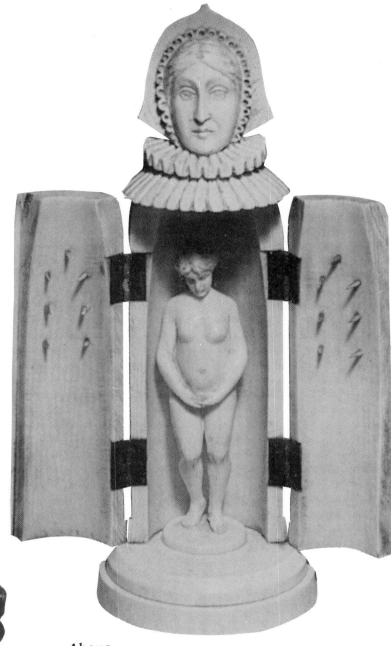

Left
French 'real photograph' risqué postcard, circa 1905.

Below
'Iphigenia', a bronze and ivory figure cast and carved from a model by *Ferdinand Preiss*, of a maiden leaning against a dark patinated rock, wearing a gold patinated dress revealing her right breast, 29.6cm. high.
(Christie's)

Above
A carved ivory model of an iron maiden, the top surmounted by the head of a woman, above a pair of doors, enclosing a compartment with a nude female standing within, on circular stepped plinth, 20cm. high.
(Phillips)

Carlo Molani: A glazed porcelain group of an amorous couple upon a day-bed, a pekinese seated at the foot of the bed, 12" long. *(Bonhams)*

Above
A set of erotic lithographs by *Peter Fendi.*

Far Left
Manner of David: 'A Good View', oil on board, 15½" x 12", framed behind a dummy oil painting of trees on a riverbank.

Japanese ink and watercolour on a wooden board of a
concubine and dragon, signed *A. Valette*, 39.8cm. x 50cm.
(Phillips)

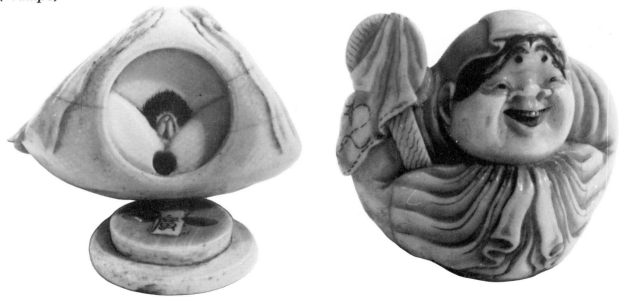

Two views of Ofuku or Okame, the goddess of eroticism and
mirth, in carved ivory.

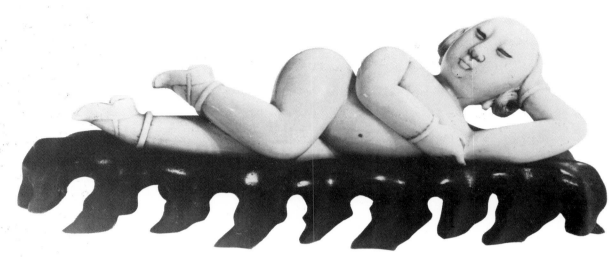

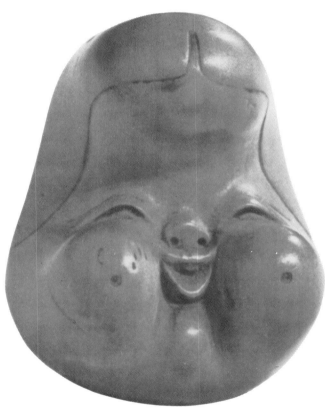

Top and left
19th century Chinese carved ivory medical figures.

Above
Carved boxwood head of Okame, Japanese goddess of eroticism, incorporating all the parts of the female body.

An erotic moulded brass box,
in the form of a day bed, the
hinged cover opening to reveal
an amorous couple.
(Bonhams)

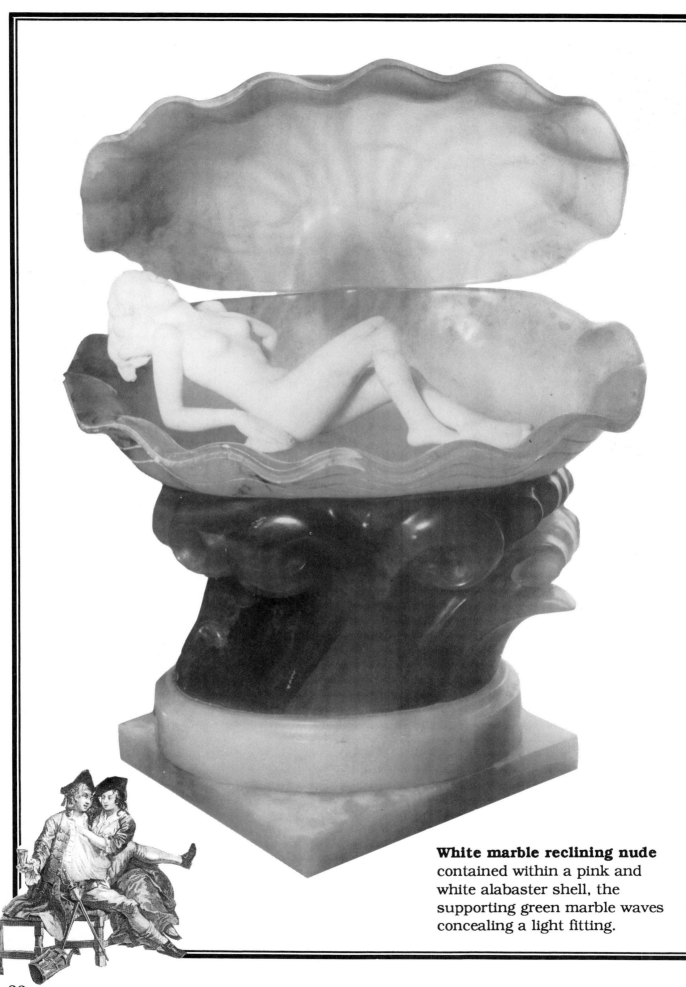

White marble reclining nude contained within a pink and white alabaster shell, the supporting green marble waves concealing a light fitting.

A large KPM Berlin rectangular plaque painted by *R. Dittrich* with scantily clad maidens emblematic of the five senses standing amongst tropical plants, *blue beehive mark,* 11¹/₄" high x 19" wide, 19th century.

Below
Bronze door knocker by *Moorland*, the male figure hinged in order to rise and fall when operative.

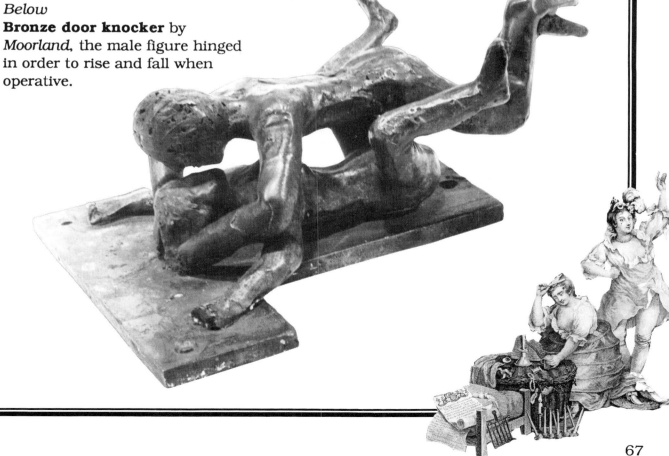

A Chinese scroll containing twelve erotic scenes of lovers and groups in interiors and garden landscapes, watercolour and ink on silk, each panel 8³/₄" x 7³/₄". *(Bonhams)*

A Japanese fan, painted in colours with two women conversing in a garden landscape, the reverse with three erotic episodes, 12" radius. *(Bonhams)*

A Chinese painted plaster group of a seated embracing couple, he in purple, she in pink, moulded male and female genitalia to the base, 4" high. *(Bonhams)*

**'Les Compagnons de la
Belle Table'**, a menu cover,
by *Louis Icart*, etching and
drypoint, printed in colours,
artist's proof, signed lower
right, 8" x 5½".
(Christie's)

**'Dancing Satyr and Nymph',
a dark patinated bronze
group**, cast from a model by
Bruno Zach, both standing on
tip-toe, one leg kicking
forwards, the satyr with his
arm around the woman,
36cm. high.
(Christie's)

Below
'The Bather', a silver patinated bronze figure cast from a model by *R. Abel Philippe*, of a stylised naked maiden kneeling on one knee on a rectangular pedestal, holding up a patterned drape, 51.2cm. high. *(Christie's)*

An opaque glass bottle with a frieze of nude figures and a stopper in the form of a kneeling nude by *René Lalique*, circa 1925.
Overpage
Early 19th century French erotic print *'Mon Empereur C'est La Cantiniere Du 2eme Hussard'.* *(Bonhams)*

Mon Empereur! c'est la

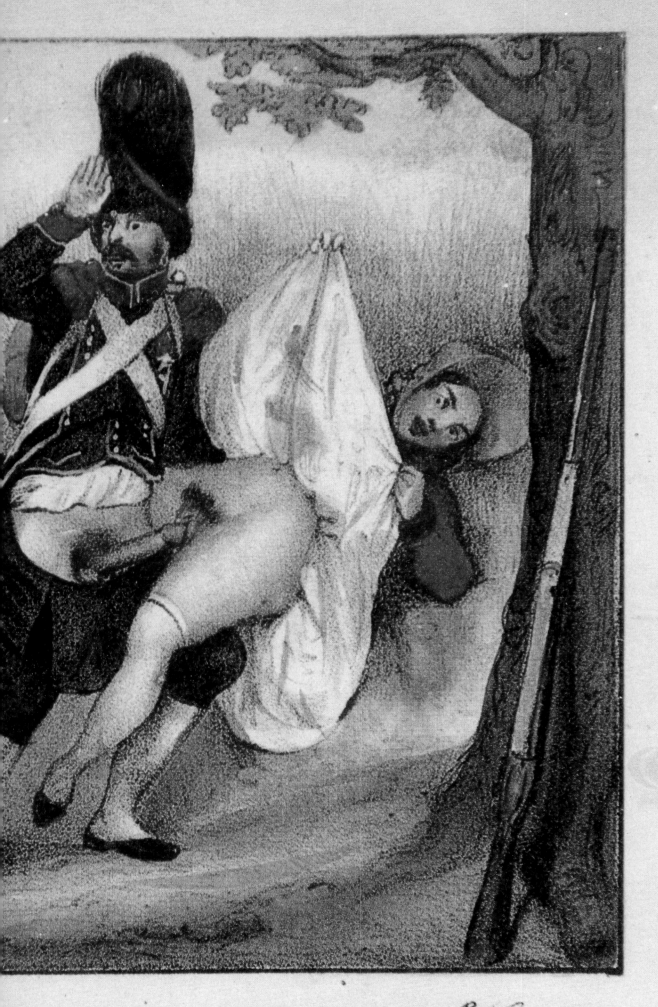

...ntiniere du 2eme Hussard.

18th century Japanese five case, black and gold lacquer, inro with 19th century carved ivory erotic figures within. Inros were worn hanging from the belt beside the sword and were used by men for carrying their family seal, medicine or tobacco.

Right
A bronze and ivory figure cast and carved from a model by *Bruno Zach*, of a topless dancing girl, her costume painted in green, red, gold and silver.
(Christie's)

Centre
A tusk, the length carved with eight amorous couples in various positions, surrounded by scrolling leaves, 18½" long.
(Bonhams)

Below
An Indian brass erotic group of an amorous couple in a position from the *Kama Sutra*, 3" high.
(Bonhams)

Right
'Egyptian Dancer', a gilt bronze figure cast from a model by *Demêtre Chiparus*, the young woman wearing a brief tasselled wrap and Egyptian headdress, poised on her toes with arms held high, 21½" high.
(Bonhams)

A European lead alloy plaque, moulded in relief with a period ménage a trois, 7" x 6".
(Bonhams)

'Dancing Girls', a pair of ivory figures, carved from models by *Ferdinand Preiss*, of striding naked young girls, both on rectangular green and black onyx bases, 13.5cm. high. *(Christie's)*

78

Right

A carved ivory phallus of large size, the heavily veined shaft engraved with two partly-clothed women bathing and depicting the phallus in use, and the base carved with female genitalia, 9½" tall, contained in a fitted box bearing the legend *This Box Contains Happiness*. (Bonhams)

Below

A massive Meerschaum pipe, the bowl carved with the figure of a scantily dressed young maiden carrying baskets, her hair adorned with flowers, shells and feathers. (Christie's)

Indian School 'Trio on a green Chaise-Longue', oil on card, framed, 10³/₄" x 12³/₄".
(*Bonhams*)

Right
An erotic Chinese bone carving of a gourd, the base removing to reveal an entwined amorous couple lying upon their sides, the gourd 2³/₄" high.
(*Bonhams*)

Far right
A small Indian portrait on ivory depicting a young woman naked to the waist, combing her hair, 3¹/₄" x 5".
(*Bonhams*)

80

Right
A Nepalese pillow album, the wood covers painted in red and yellow, folding out to reveal four amorous couples in acrobatic positions and twelve panels of script, watercolour heightened with white, each panel 7$\frac{1}{4}$" x 3$\frac{1}{4}$". *(Bonhams)*

Below
A Hindu wood panel, pierced and carved in relief with the standing figure of Krishna in a bower above a relief panel of an amorous couple, he lying on top, 8$\frac{1}{2}$" high. *(Bonhams)*

Above
French erotic plaque depicting an orgy scene, circa 1910.

Right
A stylish Hagenauer carved wood and metal figure in the form of a slender female with curly hair, otherwise naked, she rests on a rectangular flat-metal base.
(Phillips)

Left
European miniature porcelain group of an amorous couple, the woman clinging to the back of her partner.
(Bonhams)

Below
A Mennecy group of a milkmaid and her lover, she with one arm raised in alarm, a pitcher overturned at her side, her lover seated at her feet and fondling her knees, 14cm. high.
(Christie's)

Above
A European porcelain figure of a young woman seated with a drawing upon her lap, a cat emerging from her skirt, her genitalia revealed underneath the base, 2¹/₃" high.
(Bonhams)

Top left
European miniature porcelain group of an amorous couple, 1¹/₂" high.
(Bonhams)

Left
Porcelain group of a pair of ardent lovers.
(Bonhams)

Left
Franz Bergman: a cold painted erotic bronze figure of a Buddha seated on a rectangular lotus throne, the articulated body opening to reveal a painted and gilt seated nude female figure, 5¹/₂" high. *(Bonhams)*

Right
Chinese erotic horn figure with skirt raised partially baring her thigh, circa 1800, 4¹/₂" high. *(Christie's)*

Left and Below
Japanese ivory figurines of Ofuku or Okame the goddess of mirth and eroticism. In one she holds the nose of an old man, in the other the nose of an octopus, laughing because they remind her of a penis.

山の津に
入る虫の
いのがけり
　　ゆめ
　　　くら
　　　く
大しもとの宿
　　　くる

風流玄八景
行燈夕照

Attributed to Harunobu, a shunga print, with a couple making love, while another half-disrobed woman looks on, from the set *Furyu zashiki hakkei*, 20.5cm. x 27.5cm.
(Christie's)

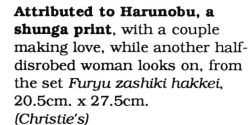

Japanese porcelain erotic figural group, 19th century, reclining nude mother with suckling baby, 9¼" wide, on a rectangular wooden stand.
(Skinner Inc)

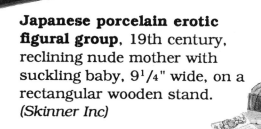

Above and right
Two erotic rectangular cast bronzed metal plaques depicting amorous couples, 3" x 2¹/₄", each inscribed *EY*. *(Bonhams)*

Left
A circular bronze medallion, decorated in low relief with a nun and two monks, 1³/₄" diameter. *(Bonhams)*

Right
A European bronzed metal figure of a seated girl dressed in peasant's costume with headscarf, the underside revealing her genitalia, 2¹/₄" high. *(Bonhams)*

Right
A large ivory phallus, the end
mounted in embossed silver with a
scene of two seated women being
serenaded in a garden landscape,
10^1/$_4$" long.
(Bonhams)

Below
'Bacchantes', a Lalique glass vase of
flared cylindrical form, the clear and
satin-finished glass moulded in relief
with nude female dancing figures, with
engraved signature, *R. Lalique, France*,
24.5cm. high.
(Christie's)

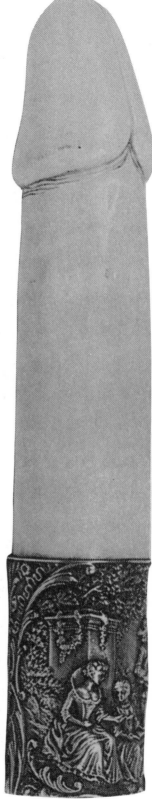

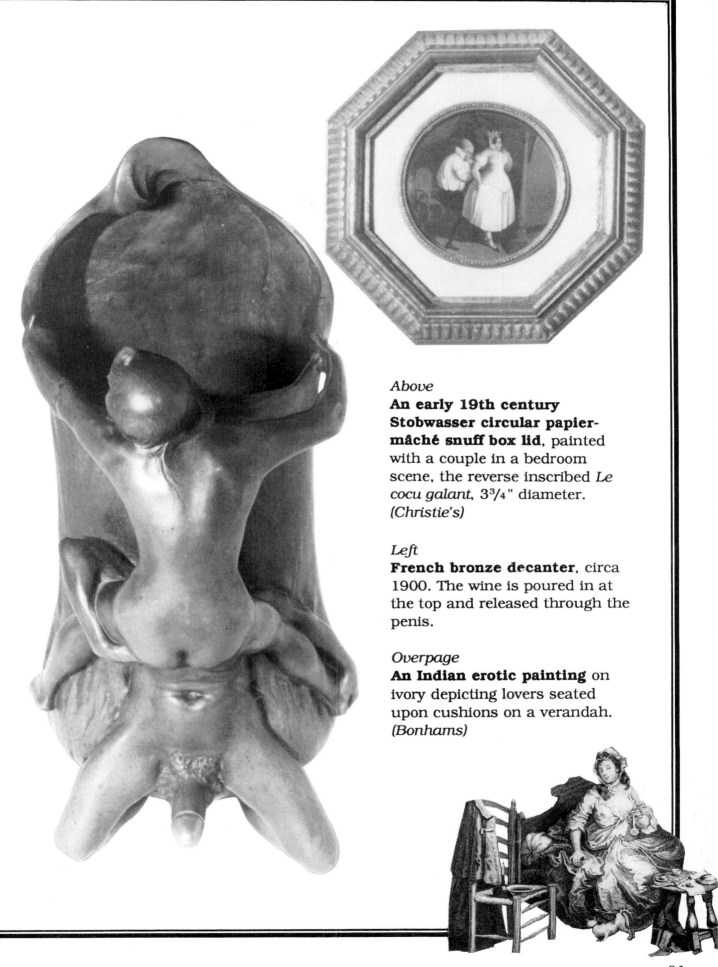

Above

An early 19th century Stobwasser circular papier-mâché snuff box lid, painted with a couple in a bedroom scene, the reverse inscribed *Le cocu galant*, 3³/₄" diameter. *(Christie's)*

Left

French bronze decanter, circa 1900. The wine is poured in at the top and released through the penis.

Overpage

An Indian erotic painting on ivory depicting lovers seated upon cushions on a verandah. *(Bonhams)*

A late 19th century bronze group of a young harvester with rake, the stacked wheat sheaves at his side concealing a naked, seated young maiden, entitled *The Harvester*, 6" high. (Christie's)

Right
An erotic print by *Aubrey Vincent Beardsley* (1872-1898)

Below
19th century European patch-box with painted decoration on both sides of the lid, the interior having a scene of love-making.

Above
Two 19th century lithophane miniature panels depicting an amorous artist and his model, 2¹/₃" x 2", and amorous monks and a nun in a monastery interior, 2¹/₄" x 1³/₄", boxed. *(Bonhams)*

Left
'The Tambourine', a hand coloured print by *Thomas Rowlandson.*

Above right
A European bronze figure of a flying phallus, mounted by a nymph, 6¹/₂" long. *(Bonhams)*

Right
Raymond Hesse: Scenes des Maisons d'Illusions, published Paris, 1929, illustrations by *Leon Courbouleix*, morocco backed paper covered boards, with thirty-eight plates and five additional illustrations. *(Bonhams)*

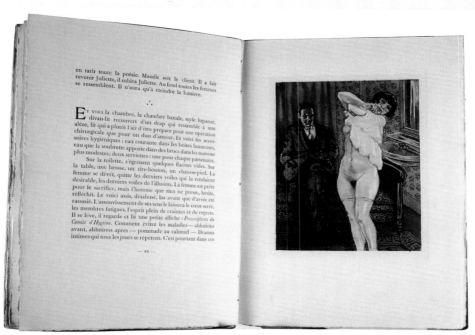

en tarir toute la poésie. Maudit soit le client. Il a fait revenir Juliette, il subira Juliette. Au fond toutes les femmes se ressemblent. Il n'aura qu'à éteindre la lumière.

∴

Et voici la chambre, la chambre banale, style lupanar, divan-lit recouvert d'un drap qui ressemble à une alèze, lit qui a plutôt l'air d'être préparé pour une opération chirurgicale que pour un duo d'amour. Et voici les accessoires hygiéniques : eau courante dans des boîtes luxueuses, eau que la soubrette apporte dans des brocs dans les maisons plus modestes; deux serviettes : une pour chaque partenaire.

Sur la toilette, s'égrènent quelques flacons vides. Sur la table, une brosse, un tire-bouton, un chausse-pied. La femme se dévêt, quitte les derniers voiles qui la rendaient désirable, les derniers voiles de l'illusion. La femme est prête pour le sacrifice, mais l'homme que rien ne presse, hésite, réfléchit. Le voici assis, désabusé, las avant que d'avoir été rassasié. L'assouvissement de ses sens le laissera le cœur serré, les membres fatigués, l'esprit plein de craintes et de regrets. Il se lève, il regarde et lit une petite affiche : *Prescriptions du Comité d'Hygiène*. Comment éviter les maladies — ablutions avant, ablutions après — pommade au calomel — Drames intimes qui tous les jours se répètent. C'est pourtant dans ces

— 22 —

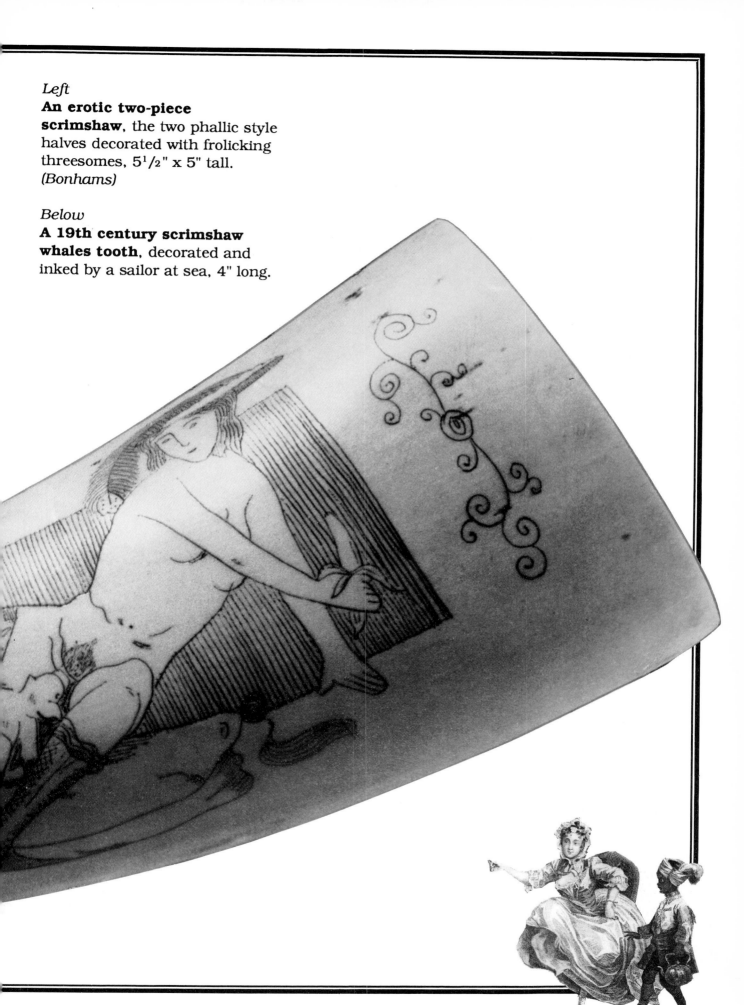

Left
An erotic two-piece scrimshaw, the two phallic style halves decorated with frolicking threesomes, 5^1/$_2$" x 5" tall. *(Bonhams)*

Below
A 19th century scrimshaw whales tooth, decorated and inked by a sailor at sea, 4" long.

Top left
Indian erotic scenes
depicting amorous couples in
various positions within
curtained interiors, each
scene with inscriptions on
reverse. *(Bonhams)*

Left
**A famille rose 'Surprise'
punch bowl**, the interior
painted with a lady and male
companion in a garden, the
exterior with numerous
ladies involved in music
making and other activities
by a pavilion, the base with a
couple involved in an erotic
scene, 15" diameter, 18th
century. *(Bonhams)*

Right
**An unusual hardstone-
inlaid erotic sliding panel**,
circa 1800, set with coloured
hardstones on painted silk,
depicting figures beside a
pavilion and on terraces, the
panel removable and
revealing an erotic scene set
on a terrace, $10^{1}/_{4}$" x 8"
overall. *(Christie's)*

Below
An Indian bone panel carved
in relief with an amorous
couple wearing elaborate
headdresses in an interior,
framed by peacocks, $7^{1}/_{4}$"
long. *(Bonhams)*

Above

A Lalique frosted glass pendant of rectangular section moulded in relief with two angels facing each other and holding hands, with sepia staining, 3³/₄" high. *(Christie's)*

Franz Bergman: a cold painted erotic bronze figure of an Egyptian Sarcophagus embellished with hieroglyphics, the case opening to reveal a gilded, standing nude female figure, arms crossed over her breasts, on a rectangular veined marble base, 9" high, signed *Nam Greb. (Bonhams)*

A Swiss gold and enamel bridgecock verge watch with secret erotic panel depicting a priest and a country girl, the gilt movement signed *Fournier A Genève*, 55mm. diameter. *(Christie's)*

Above
'O Mighty Woman!', a bronze group cast from a model by *J.J. Nielsons*, the female nude stands contraposto, hands on hips, on a naturalistic base, her distraught lover at her feet, 14½" high. *(Christie's)*

Left
Ivory figure of Napoleon suffering from piles on the eve of the Battle of Waterloo, English circa 1830.

Left
A European cast iron relief panel depicting an amorous couple upon a day-bed in an interior, 6" x 4¼". *(Bonhams)*

Below
A rare early 20th century German life-size bronze statue of a male nude struggling with a serpent, cast from a model by *Arthur Lewin-Funcke.* *(Christie's)*

Right
A European cold cast bronze group of Leda and the Swan in amorous union, 8¼" high. *(Bonhams)*

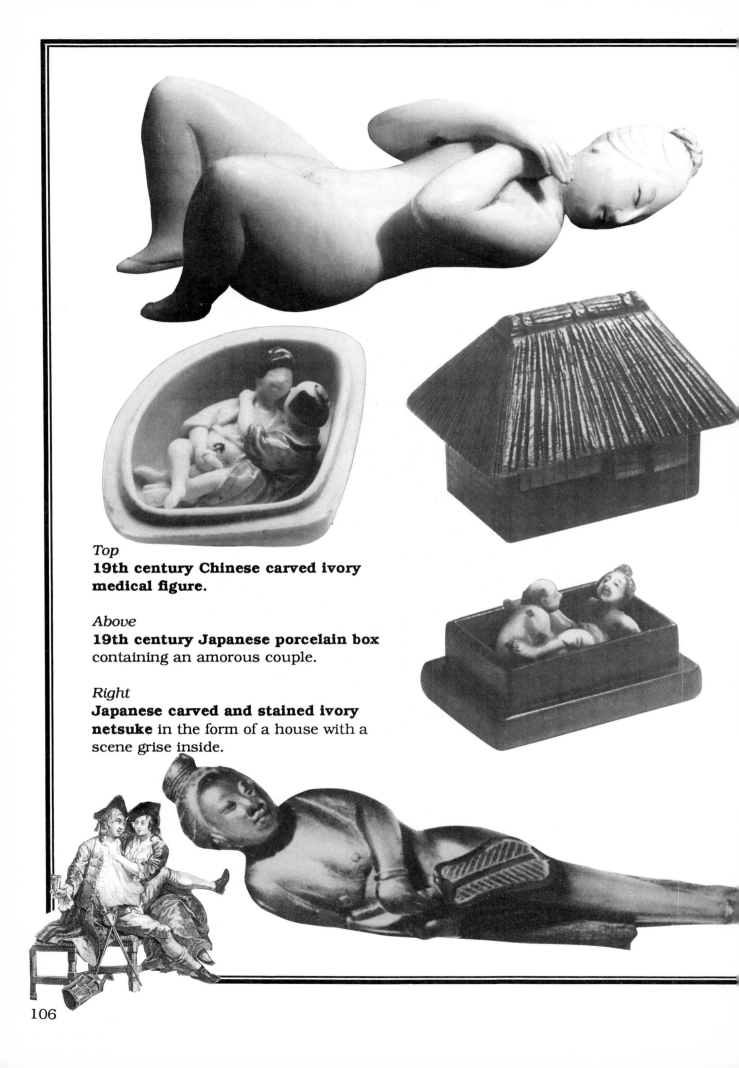

Top
19th century Chinese carved ivory medical figure.

Above
19th century Japanese porcelain box containing an amorous couple.

Right
Japanese carved and stained ivory netsuke in the form of a house with a scene grise inside.

**An early 19th century Indian
miniature painting** on ivory of
an erotic scene.
Left
Chinese erotic horn figure of a
semi naked woman holding a fan
in her left hand, 4¼" high, circa
1800. *(Christie's)*

A German oval metal dish, cast in relief with an amorous couple upon a day-bed, the border with Greek key motif, 5" long. *(Bonhams)*

Below
'Suzanne', a Lalique opalescent figurine, of a naked maiden, her arms outstretched and holding her robes, 23cm. high. *(Christie's)*

Right
'Nature revealing herself to Science', a gilt bronze and silver-patinated figure cast from a model by *L.E. Barrias*, of a maiden clad in a long dress and shawl, her breasts revealed, 43.2cm. high *(Christie's)*

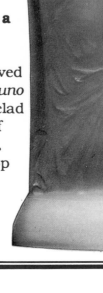

Above
'The Riding Crop', a dark patinated bronze and ivory figure cast and carved from a model by *Bruno Zach*, of a scantily clad maiden with a scarf tied below her bust, holding a riding crop behind her back, 32cm. high. *(Christie's)*

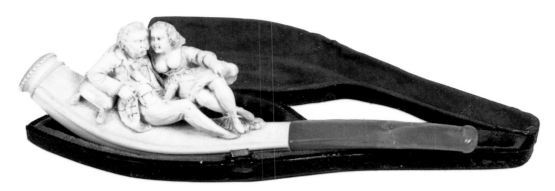

Above

A carved Meerschaum cheroot holder modelled with an amorous couple in period dress reclining upon a cushion, 5³/₄" long.
(Bonhams)

Above

A shell-shaped carved and engraved mother-of-pearl plaque depicting an amorous monk approaching a lady reclining beneath a tree, the reverse engraved with an amorous couple and a third figure seated in a grotto, 3¹/₂" wide, cased.
(Bonhams)

Left
'Blue Buddha', by *Louis Icart*, etching and drypoint, printed in colours, signed lower right, *Copyright 1924 by Les Graveurs Modernes, 194 Rue de Rivoli, Paris*, 17" x 21¼". *(Christie's)*

Below left
A white marble figure of a reclining maiden, by *C. Baribella*, 70cm. long. *(Spencers)*

Right
Late 19th century figure of Juro, the god of longevity, traditionally depicted with a long head in the shape of a penis.

Far right
A gilt bronze figure of a girl, cast from a model by *Lorenzl*, poised naked above an oval green onyx base, 37cm. high. *(Phillips)*

Overpage
**'Les Délassements d'Eros',
erotic watercolour** by *Gerda Wegener*, on card, 18cm. wide.
(Christie's)

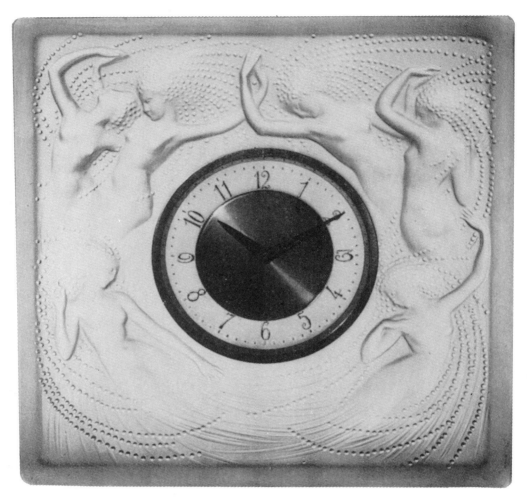

'Sirènes', a Lalique satin-finished glass clock, the square body moulded with six naked sea sprites, with a circular clock, Arabic chapters, 28cm. high.
(Christie's)

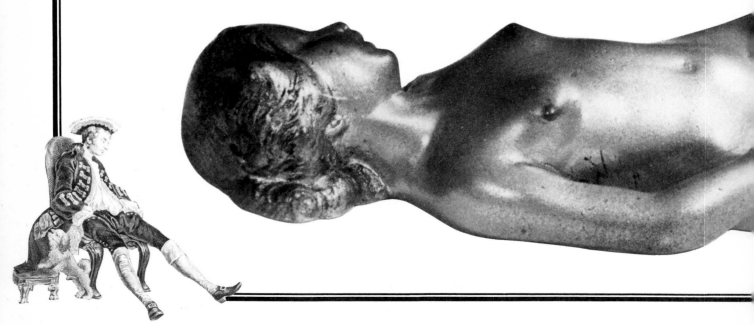

Above
'Dancing Girls', by Le Faguays, a silver-plated bronze group of two nude female figures, on an illuminated marble base, 21" high.
(Christie's)

Below
French gilt bronze female reclining figure, circa 1900.

Below

19th century Chinese porcelain bowls, the rust coloured exteriors gilded with stylised birds, the lids painted inside with amorous couples, 4¹/₂" and 4" high. *(Bonhams)*

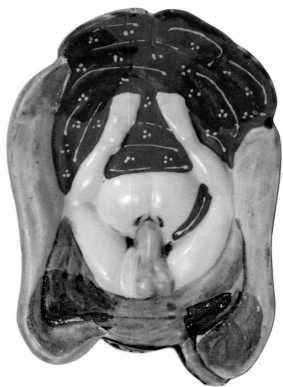

Top left
Indian miniature painting on ivory depicting Krishna being received by a willing devotee. *(Bonhams)*

Above
A Chinese porcelain group of a seated embracing couple in floral kimonos, painted in colours and gilded, with male and female genitalia upon the base, ·3¹/₂" high. *(Bonhams)*

Left
An Indian painting of a lady reclining on her day-bed with her hand maidens in attendance, with elaborate borders of red and green decorated with pansies, 14cm. x 9cm. *(Bonhams)*

Right
**Chinese neolithic earthenware
lung shan** in the form of breasts.

Below
'Sea Maiden', a bronze statue
cast from a model by *Rossi* of a
naked maiden lying on the crest
of wave, a fearless seagull below
her, 55cm. high.
(Christie's)

Right
A Sabino opalescent dish, the reserve heavily moulded with three naked swimming maidens, 38.4cm. diameter.
(Christie's)

Below
19th century German Meerschaum pipe decorated with a carving of a copulating couple.

Above
Three carved phalli, in wood, and inscribed bone, two containing a rattle, both approx. 7" long, and the third in bone, inscribed, 5³/₄"long.
(Bonhams)

Above
Franz, Marquis Von Bayros: 'Gotterliebschaften'.
(Bonhams)

Above
**'What's on a man's mind', an
ivorine head** composed of lithe
female bodies entwined to create
a face, with sculptured hair and
an erotic scene, 3½" high.
(Bonhams)

Below
Art Nouveau gilt-bronze group
depicting a naked girl with
poppies in her hair, swept up by
a wave, pursued by a naked
male. This dish is of mottled
ochre and red marble.

Right
A metal figural double dish
from a model by *Max Blondat*
featuring a naked girl and boy
sitting and embracing, signed
and stamped.
(Phillips)

122

Top
Art Nouveau gilt bronze figure of a naked seated woman proposing a toast.
(Bonhams)

Above
Late 18th century, French school, erotic etching, 3½" x 2½".
(Bonhams)

Right
European bronze group of a satyr and his lover.
(Bonhams)

Left
'Love on a bicycle' by *Thomas Rowlandson*, one of a series depicting couples making love in various states of locomotion.

Below
'A soft and pleasing place', signed watercolour by *Eugene Delausy*, 6" x 9½". *(Bonhams)*

125

Above
Study for 'La Nuit et le Moment', by *Louis Icart*, ink and watercolour on paper, signed lower right, 9" x 7".
(Christie's)

Right
Fibreglass lamp cast from an electric light bulb in the form of a nipple by *Uwe Zimmer*.

Above
19th century English shell cameo carved with an amorous couple, in a gold frame, 1½" high.

Left
Bronze figure of a woman clutching a robe to her body by *G. Chauvel*, circa 1900, made as an advertisement for *Bain de Champagne Caron*.

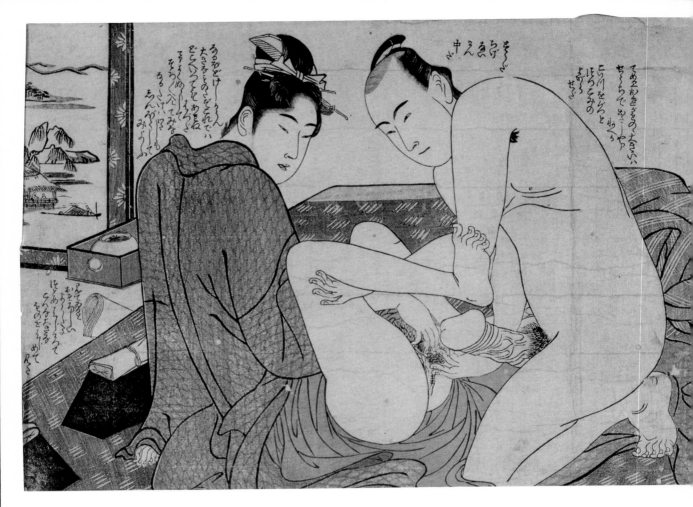

Above
After Utamaro: An erotic woodcut print on paper depicting an amorous couple upon a green carpet before a window revealing mountainous landscape, 15" x 10" *(Bonhams)*

Right
A Chinese carved bone gourd engraved and stained with two men in an interior and inscribed, the base removing to reveal a seated amorous couple, the gourd 2¹/₂" high. *(Bonhams)*

Far right
A famille rose Surprise bowl, the interior painted with a couple by a low fence, the exterior with figural cartouches on a moulded petal spray and dotted ground, the base with figures and animals involved in erotic activity, 10¹/₄" diameter, 18th century. *(Bonhams)*

Above
A painted ivory Oni, of an
amorous couple in the
missionary position, 2¹/₂" long.
(Bonhams)

Right
A stained ivory netsuke, of a
rabbit being taken from behind
doggy style by another smaller
rabbit, 1¹/₂" long.
(Bonhams)

Un roué.

235

DÉPOSÉ DANS TOUS LES PAYS

Alpha series fantasy postcard, circa
1905, entitled *'Un roué'*.
(Border Bygones)

Right
**'Scarf Dancer', a
bronze figure** cast
from a model by *Louis-
Ernest Barrias*, of a
naked maiden
standing tip-toe on one
leg, her head thrown
back, holding a gilded
scarf over her left
shoulder, 61.5cm.
high.
(Christie's)

Far right
Carved ivory dildo on
a marble base by
Wiener Werkstätte,
circa 1910.

Overpage
'Leda and the Swan' by *Louis
Icart*, etching and drypoint,
printed in colours, signed lower
right, with artist's blindstamp,
1934. *(Christie's)*

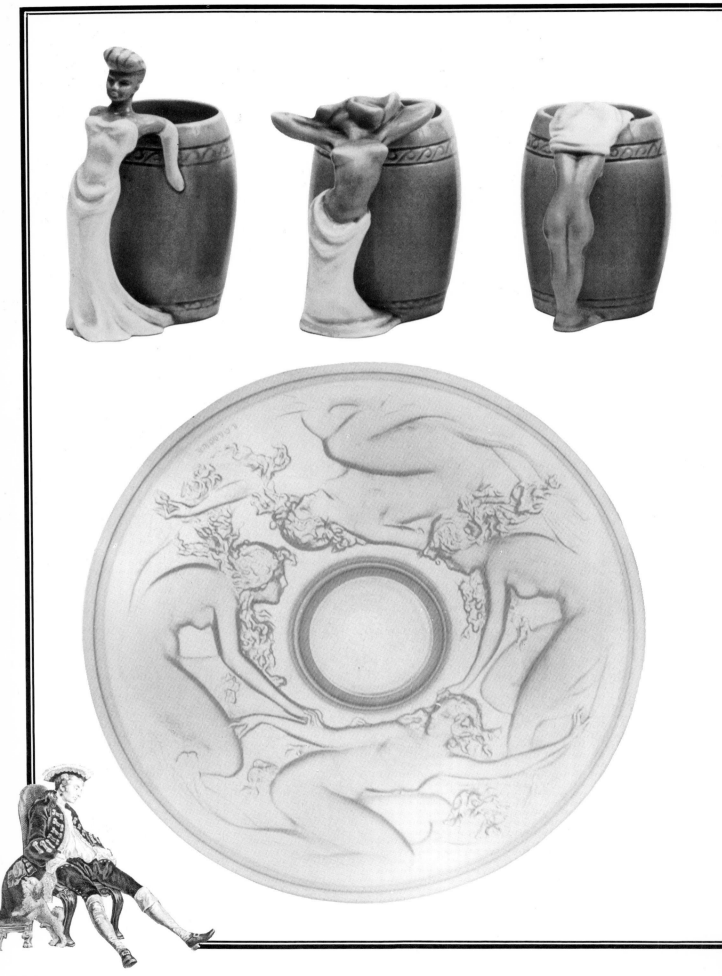

Above

A set of six Kindell Pottery barrel-shaped mugs, the handles modelled in the form of a lissom young woman in various stages of undress and abandonment, 12.5-16cm. high, 1940s. *(Sothebys)*

Left

'Quatre Sirènes', a blue tinted Lalique glass encrier, 60cm. diameter. *(Spencers)*

A late 19th century bronze group, of a reclining woman with her skirts up around her waist, before a kneeling man with open breeches, upon rectangular base, 6¹/₂" long. *(Bonhams)*

The Gallop

'The Gallop', a hand coloured
print by *Thomas Rowlandson*,
(1757-1827).

Right
An Indian brass erotic group of an
amorous couple in a position from
the *Kama Sutra*.
(Bonhams)

Right
A small musical erotic automaton, Swiss, first quarter 19th century, with hinged base and cover opening to reveal enamel scene of an amorous threesome, the gilt movement playing a tune on 8-tooth comb with pinned barrel, 37mm. long.
(Christie's)

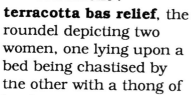

Below
'Chastisement': terracotta bas relief, the roundel depicting two women, one lying upon a bed being chastised by the other with a thong of birch twigs, 6½" diameter.
(Bonhams)

'The Monk and the Dairymaid', an English 19th century bronze group varying in naughtiness according to the angle from which it is viewed.

138

Above

Vesta case, or matchbox, French 1883-5, made of silver with blue enamel decoration, depicting two women, stripped to the waist, duelling.

Left

A French Art Deco ceramic figure modelled as a nude girl wearing a golden skull cap, 34cm. high, signed *Edition Kaza France*, on base
(Phillips)

Above
'Fat People I' oil on board by *W. Botten*, 9" x 23".
(Bonhams)

Right
'Bacchantes', a Lalique opalescent vase, the flared cylindrical body moulded in relief with nude female dancing figures, 24.5cm. high.
(Christie's)

A carved ivory group, of an amorous couple preparing for oral love, upon rectangular horn base, 5" high. (Bonhams)

Left
Art Nouveau gilded bronze female nude figure wearing a necklace.

Above
Bronze figure of a monkey in an excited state, with articulated arm.

Right
19th century scrimshaw whale's tooth decorated with an erotic scene, 4" long.

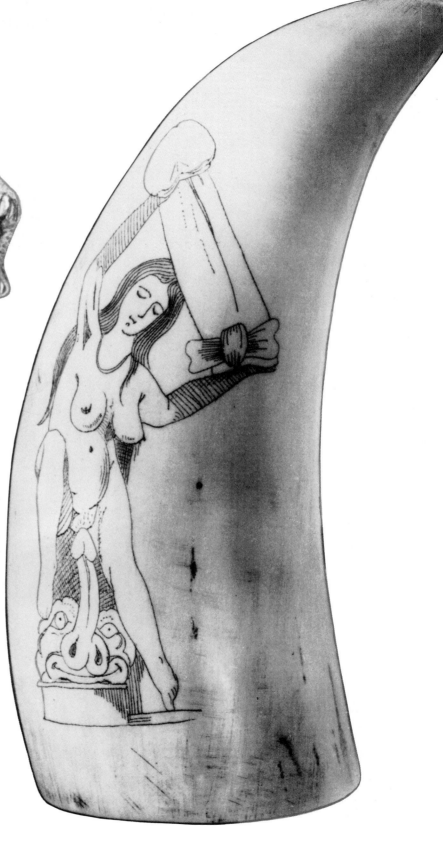

Above

An attractive enamelled rectangular box, the top depicting a naked woman resting in an ethereal setting being showered from above with golden coins, 9cm. wide, marked *935*.
(Phillips)

Right

A German enamelled cigarette case depicting a young girl wearing a lacy nightdress falling from one shoulder, 9cm. long, stamped *935*.
(Phillips)

A good carved and stained ivory erotic chess set, comprising sixteen phallus pawns and the 'men' formed as amorous naked couples, pawns 2¹/₂", 'men' approximately 3¹/₂", European, circa 1925.
(Bonhams)

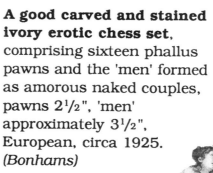

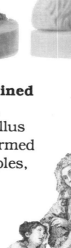

Above
A Chinese porcelain famille rose box and cover, decorated with a court scene, the reverse revealing an erotic interior scene, 7½" wide.
(Bonhams)

Below
Chinese porcelain groups of amorous couples in various athletic positions.
(Bonhams)

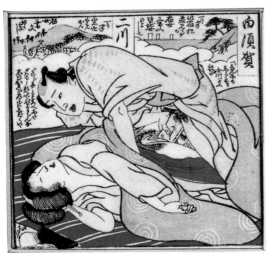

Japanese coloured woodblock prints depicting amorous couples in various positions in an interior before a village landscape, each print 4¹/₂" square.
(Bonhams)

'Leda and the Swan', a bronze plaque by *André Lavrillier*.

Above
Medieval dice, in the form of male and female figures, carved from cubes of ivory.

Left
Nessus and Deianira, Italian bronze group, 17th century.

147

Above
A carved Meerschaum cheroot holder modelled as *Leda and the Swan* in an amorous embrace.
(Bonhams)

Above right
19th century German cast metal roundel depicting a gnome engaged in sexual activities.
(Bonhams)

Right
'One Down, Nine Hundred and Ninety Nine To Go', colour lithograph by *Icart*, 6½" x 5",
(Bonhams)

Above
'Overlooked', a 19th century hand coloured erotic engraving.
(Bonhams)

Left
Indian brass group of a couple in a position from the *Kama Sutra*.
(Bonhams)

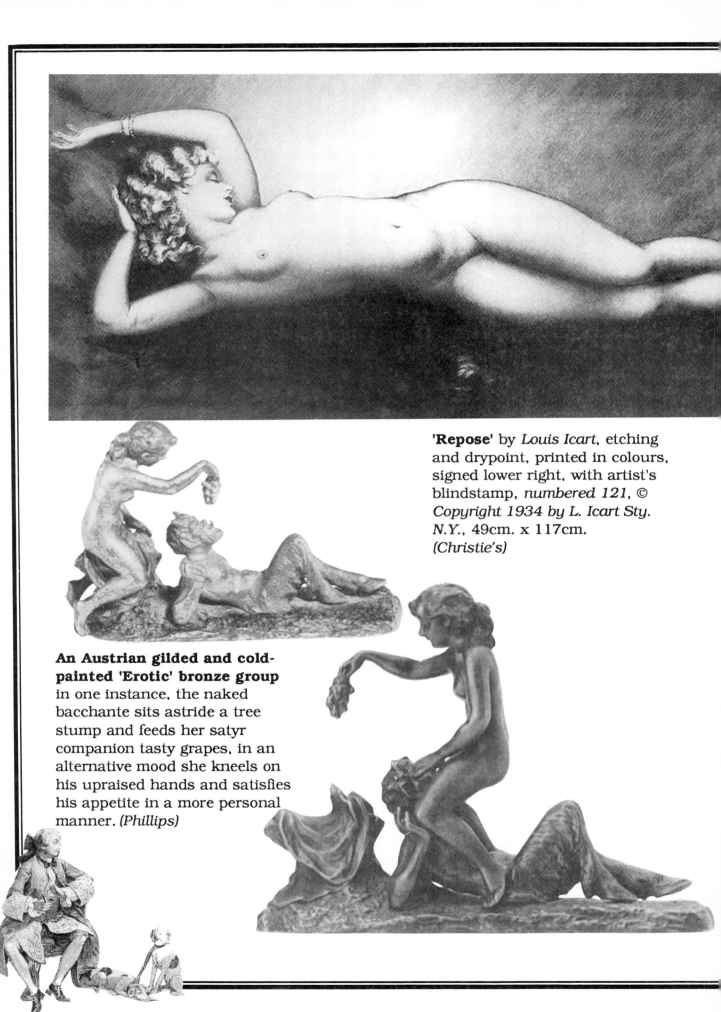

'Repose' by *Louis Icart*, etching and drypoint, printed in colours, signed lower right, with artist's blindstamp, *numbered 121, © Copyright 1934 by L. Icart Sty. N.Y., 49cm. x 117cm. (Christie's)*

An Austrian gilded and cold-painted 'Erotic' bronze group in one instance, the naked bacchante sits astride a tree stump and feeds her satyr companion tasty grapes, in an alternative mood she kneels on his upraised hands and satisfies his appetite in a more personal manner. *(Phillips)*

Right
'Flower Girl', a gilt-bronze Art Nouveau table-lamp, cast from a model by *Louis Chalon*, of a maiden wearing a long flowing dress and holding out a lamp under a flowerholder, 40cm. high. *(Christie's)*

Below
Pâte de verre vase, moulded in brown and beige with two seated nudes.

Overpage
'The Concert', a hand coloured print by *Thomas Rowlandson*, (1757-1827).

Left
'Like a Whirlwind' by *H. Rudolf*,
etching signed in pencil.
(Bonhams)

Below
**20th century School: 'The Big
Mamma'**, a bedroom scene with
a young man and his buxom
Negress teacher, watercolour,
9" x 6½".
(Bonhams)

Above
**Photogravure of
'Erotic Acrobats'** by
Peter Fendi, 8" x 5".
(Bonhams)

Left
**18th century erotic
sepia engraving** by
Borell.

155

Above
Indian miniature erotic scenes depicting amorous couples in various positions within a contained interior, each scene with inscriptions on reverse, oil and gold paint on paper, contained within two wood panels, painted on both sides with similar scenes, 7½" x 2½".
(Bonhams)

Right
A bronzed metal hexagonal teapot, the side panels depicting amorous couples in interior and garden scenes, 7" high.
(Bonhams)

A Nepalese pillow album, the wood covers folding out to reveal twelve amorous couples in various positions within curtained interiors, watercolour heightened with white and gold, each panel 18cm. x 8cm. *(Bonhams)*

Two erotic Japanese miniature painted plaster plaques, one depicting an entwined amorous couple, the other a seated woman in a red skirt, each 2" x 1¼", contained in a cloth covered box.

Above
A good and large whalebone plaque, the centre stained and engraved with a Classical style scene depicting a satyr and his nude female lover in a wooded mountainous landscape, 9³/₄" x 18".
(Bonhams)

Right
'Spanish Maiden', a bronze figure cast from a model by *Bruno Zach* of a standing maiden with her hands on her hips, wearing a short strapless dress and a shawl, 30.4cm. high.
(Christie's)

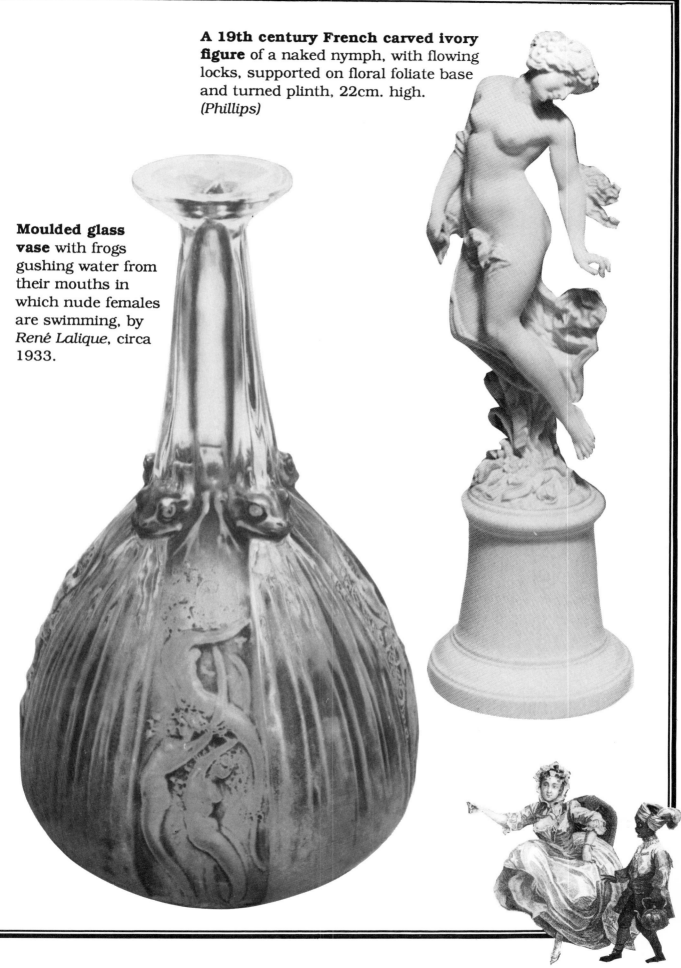

A 19th century French carved ivory figure of a naked nymph, with flowing locks, supported on floral foliate base and turned plinth, 22cm. high. *(Phillips)*

Moulded glass vase with frogs gushing water from their mouths in which nude females are swimming, by *René Lalique*, circa 1933.

Museums:
Museo Nazionale (Bargello), Florence
Prague National Gallery, Prague
Tate Gallery, London
Victoria & Albert Museum, London

Private Owners, Dealers & Auction Houses
Antiques by Constantine, New Bond Street, London W1
Victor Arwas Esq., London
Bonhams Chelsea, 65-69 Lots Road, Chelsea, London SW10 0RN
Bonhams, Montpelier Galleries, Montpelier Street, London SW7 1HH
Border Bygones, The Vallets, Forge Crossing, Lyonshall, Kington,
    HR5 3JQ
Christie's (International) SA, 8 place de la Taconnerie, 1204 Geneva,
    Switzerland
Christie's (Monaco) S A M, Park Place, 98000 Monte Carlo, Monaco
Christie's Scotland, 164-166 Bath Street, Glasgow
Christie's South Kensington, 85 Old Brompton Road, London
    SW7 3LD
Christie's, 8 King Street, St James's, London SW1Y 6QT
Christie's East, 219 East 67th Street, New York NY 10021, USA
Christie's, 502 Park Avenue, New York 10022, USA
Christie's, Cornelis Schuystraat 57, 1071 JG Amsterdam,
    Netherlands
Christie's SA Roma, 114 Piazza Navona, 00186 Rome
Christie's SWIRE, 1202 Alexandra House, 16-20 Charter Road,
    Hong Kong
Sylvia Collins, The Antique Centre, New Bond Street, London
Davies & Hales, Antiquarians, Kings Road, London SW3
Editions Graphiques, Clifford Street, London W1
Sven Gahlin, Esq., Sevrington, Kent
Geering & Colyer (Black Horse Agencies), Highgate, Hawkhurst, Kent
Peter Lodge, Esq., London
Lords Gallery, Wellington Road, London NW8
Lots Road Galleries, 71 Lots Road, Chelsea, London SW10 0RN
Massada Antiques, The Antique Centre, New Bond Street,
    London W1
Rod McLennan, Harwood Road, London SW6
Obelisk Gallery, Crawford Street, London W1
Phillips Manchester, Trinity House, 114 Northenden Road, Sale,
    Manchester
Phillips Son & Neale, SA, 10 rue des Chaudronniers, 1204 Geneva
Phillips West Two, 10 Salem Road, London W2
Phillips, 11 Bayle Parade, Folkestone, Kent
Phillips, 49 London Road, Sevenoaks, Kent
Phillips, 65 George Street, Edinburgh EH2 2JL
Phillips, Blenstock House, 7 Blenheim Street, New Bond Street,
    London W1Y 0AS
Phillips Marylebone, Hayes Place, Lisson Grove, London NW1 6UA
Phillips, New House, Christleton Road, Chester CH3 5TD
Madeleine & Elizabeth Pomper, The Antique Centre, New Bond
    Street, London W1
Skinner Inc., Bolton Gallery, Route 117, Bolton, MA, USA
Sotheby's, 34-35 New Bond Street, London W1A 2AA
Sotheby's, Summers Place, Billingshurst, Kent
Sotheby's, 1334 York Avenue, 10021 New York, USA
Henry Spencer, 40 The Square, Retford, Notts
Brian Tipping, Antiquarius, Kings Road, London SW3

'The Riding Crop'
by *Bruno Zach,*
(Christie's)